ADDRESSES ON THE
EPISTLE TO THE ROMANS

ADDRESSES ON
THE EPISTLE TO THE ROMANS

by

KENNETH BOUNDS

London
THE EPWORTH PRESS

THE EPWORTH PRESS
(FRANK H. CUMBERS)
25-35 City Road, London, E.C.1.

MELBOURNE   CAPE TOWN
NEW YORK   TORONTO

Printed in England by Page & Thomas, Ltd.
Sheraton Street, London, W.1, and at Chesham

TO

PETER, GRACE, MARGARET, JOY

WITH THE PRAYER THAT THEY MAY
ALL PREACH THE EVERLASTING GOSPEL

FOREWORD

THE Epistle to the Romans is the Book which has moved Empires because it has moved men. It was the message of this Epistle which set Martin Luther on fire for Christ. The same message set John Wesley ablaze. Eleven of his fifty-three sermons have texts taken from this Epistle, some of the titles are : Justification by Faith, Righteousness by Faith, The First Fruits of the Spirit, The Witness of the Spirit, and so on.

The early Methodists were nurtured by the message of the Letter, its message was the milk and the meat of the Revival. From time to time the ordinary Christian in the pew has told me that the Epistle to the Romans is most difficult to understand. The following addresses have been written with such people in mind. Technical words have been avoided as far as possible, but the theology of the Apostle Paul has been allowed to speak for itself. Young Christians in particular would be advised to read each chapter of the book with the corresponding chapter of the Epistle. Matters of Criticism and of Background are not dealt with, but the author has not been unmindful of them. It is certain that the Apostle Paul wrote the Epistle in the midst of a very busy life as an introduction to his own preaching and teaching. As such, we are able to gather together the main points of his theology.

I am indebted to my friends, the members of my Bible Classes, in the Harpenden and the Birstall and Birkenshaw Methodist Circuits, who have worked through the Epistle with me week by week. I express appreciation to these friends, and also to the Book Steward, the Rev. Frank H. Cumbers, B.A., B.D., for many helpful suggestions.

ONE

'PAUL . . . SLAVE . . . JESUS CHRIST . . . CALLED . . . APOSTLE
. . . SEPARATED . . . GOSPEL . . . GOD . . .'—ROM. I^1-7

WE have in this first verse of the epistle eight of the
most important words in the New Testament;
indeed, if we were to excise these words from the New
Testament there would be very little left.

Paul, what a word! To estimate how important Paul
was, try to imagine what would have happened had Saul
of Tarsus never been converted. Several years after he
had met with Christ he appears on the scene as a middle-
aged man ablaze for Christ, and from that time Christianity began to move in new channels, which ultimately
led the Church into a new vision, a deeper understanding
of the theology of Christ, and which fashioned the whole
future history of the Church of Christ.

But had anyone approached Paul and complimented
him for the contribution he made to the Church, he most
probably would have muttered, in all humility, something
about being 'the chief of sinners', and of preaching nothing
but 'Christ and Him crucified'. He was a truly humble
man with a Christ-filled heart.

He called himself a *slave*, i.e., one who was purchased at
a price and who lived in subjection to his Master. The
subjection is the result of the purchase—and Paul never
allowed himself to forget that. The folk who forget that
they have been 'bought with a price' are the ones who do

not wish to be in subjection to Christ. That is why we need to turn again and again to Calvary, and to meditate upon the amazing love of God. The words of C. T. Studd are well worth remembering : 'If Jesus Christ be God and died for me, then no sacrifice can be too great for me to make for Him'. The Apostle glories in the fact that he was a slave of Christ. Time after time he refers to the subject. He uses the term regularly, in his epistles, to introduce himself to others. 'Paul . . . the slave of Christ . . .'

Paul the slave leads us to *Jesus Christ*—the noblest task of the redeemed soul. In a very few words the slave traces the characteristics of the Master.

(*a*) He came from the seed of David; our Lord had a human ancestry and, too, he had been promised for many a long day. This is integral in the message concerning the Lord. Had He appeared in some other way, the appeal might have been greater to the immediate recipients of the revelation, but the age-long appeal would have been less. All the love and experience which lie behind such sentences as 'What a friend we have in Jesus', 'He went about doing good', could never have been formulated. Our Lord had been in no wise unknown before the incarnation, but when we see Him clothed in our humanity we see Him as He really needs to be seen by sinning humanity.

(*b*) The powerful Son of God; 'marked out', Paul says, 'designated' as the Son of God. The specific reasons he gives for this approval of Jesus are His purity of character, and His resurrection from the dead. The Godhead of the Lord had never been appreciated until after the crucifixion. He was able to break the bonds of death, and rise again in the power of an endless life. Death was looked

upon as the wages of sin, therefore when Christ rose from
the dead the purity and blamelessness of His character
were vindicated. A man without sin could not be held
by death. Who could be the conqueror of sin and death?
Certainly not a mere man, not even from the seed of
David—and so the Divinity of our Lord began to be
understood by His disciples.

(c) To this was added the generosity of the Living
Christ, which transformed all who responded to His grace.
'By whom we have received grace and apostleship.'
Who could have made Saul of Tarsus into the Apostle
Paul but God Himself?

'I was *called* . . . and you are called' we are next told.
How bitter has been the cup of many people when they
have been questioning the application of the 'dreaded
decrees'. Am I called to salvation or not? Of course
you are called—but each must decide whether he is
effectively called or not; all must ratify the call by personal
faith (confidence) in Christ, or perish. 'Whosoever will
may come' for the promise is unto you and unto your
children and to all who are afar off, even as many as the
Lord our God shall call . . . as far as His voice can reach
—and who can limit that?

But also this Paul was an *apostle*, a messenger, an envoy, ·
an ambassador. The title of an Apostle was guarded very
closely by the members of the early church. It was ·
reserved for those who had actually seen and heard Christ,
and by Him alone had been commissioned to the task of
evangelisation. Paul jealously guarded his rights here.
He claimed that all three conditions had been fulfilled on
the Damascus Road: there he had seen and heard Christ,
and had there been commissioned by Him.

Few have seen Christ as the Twelve and Paul saw Him,

but to all who have seen our Lord with the eyes of faith
and have heard His words by faith, there has come the
commission to go and tell what great things the Lord has
done for you.

The separation of Paul unto the Gospel seems to have
been a very real truth to his mind.   He tells us that he was
separated from his mother's womb.   The inference is that
he believed he had been deliberately created by God for a
specific task.   He really believed in predestination to
Christian service.   This was ratified for Saul when in
fellowship with the Church in Antioch the word of the
Lord came and said, 'separate me Barnabas and Saul for
the work whereunto I have called them'.

A faith like that makes one strong for the Lord in times
of extremity, and will cause one to be staunch for Christ in
all circumstances.   It will also lead to exploits like the
founding of Protestantism, the building up of Methodism,
and the missionary era which followed the work and
witness of William Carey.

The Gospel.   It was to that he had been separated.
The Gospel is the good news of the grace of God—our
forefathers would have called it the 'good news of the plan
of salvation', the good news of the scheme for the redemption of the sinner.   It is the incomparable message which
is needed by people everywhere; the message for which we
are hungry, even though we rebel against it.   The Gospel
centres around Christ, who is the most hated as well as the
most loved person in the universe.   To be saved by Christ
is not desirable, so thousands believe, so the Apostle was
separated (placed apart from other tasks) to endeavour to
lead people to find in Christ the eternal blessings of the
Gospel of the Son of God's love.

The last word in our text is *God*, and He is utterly
responsible for everything which our text mentions,

Paul, the slave of Jesus Christ, called, an apostle, separated unto the Gospel, is not concerned with fables. He is concerned, and that utterly, with God. The whole being of Paul, all that he thought, said, or did, and everywhere he went (after his conversion), was dominated by the consciousness of 'God'. This God, the God and Father of our Lord Jesus Christ, was the centre of his life. May that be true of us, too!

TWO

'THE JUST SHALL LIVE BY FAITH.'—ROM. I[17]

THIS text is the greatest in Protestantism. Its truth gave birth to the Reformation in the 16th century, and has guided the Reformed section of the Church of Christ since 1517. Luther used to say that the doctrine of 'justification by faith' is the article of a standing Church. It is equally true of an individual, for the Apostle told us that 'by faith ye stand'.

It is the 'just' who shall live by faith. In a Jewish mind the 'just' would mean 'the elect', those who had been chosen in the providence of God to share His blessing and His fellowship. For such people a way had been provided whereby they could be accounted righteous in the sight of the Lord. Atonement must always precede forgiveness and reconciliation; and only those who entered into the covenant could share the blessings of the righteous.

The verse is a somewhat loose translation and quotation of Hab. 2[4] where the essence of the words imply the factor of 'faithfulness'. That was the outstanding characteristic of a good Israelite—faithfulness: faithful to God and to His Law. So when Paul tells his friends that 'whatsoever is not of faith is sin', he is repeating something every conscientious Hebrew believed. Thus the just are those who have faith in God and who are faithful to His purposes. Such folk 'shall live' by faith. When we say 'we live' we imply three things; 1. that we were born; 2. that there is growth; 3. that we are coming to fruition. Similarly when we say that a Christian lives we imply these three stages of life.

(i) The birth into the Christian life is by faith in the Son of God, Who loved us and gave Himself for us. 'Except a man be born again, he cannot see the Kingdom of God', therefore the Lord could say, 'marvel not that I said unto thee, ye must be born again'. In the days of the new covenant the elect, the justified, are those who have deliberately taken the necessary steps whereby they can be born into the family of God. An unconverted Christian is a misnomer. The New Testament declares quite unequivocally that no man can become a member of the Kingdom of God except he exercise a personal faith towards our Lord Jesus Christ.

(ii) The life, too, involves a growth in grace. As in the natural life, so in the spiritual, the imbecile alone fails to grow into full manhood. No person who is a spiritual imbecile is natural; we should all grow in grace and in the knowledge of the Lord. Such a growth can only come as we perpetually exercise our faith in the Lord. Should our faith stop at justifying faith what awful specimens of Christians we would be.

(iii) This growth must lead to fruition, and the fruition of the Christian is an eternity in the fellowship of the Lord.

It is inconceivable that the life of a follower of the Lord should fail in this, for our whole salvation is based upon the death and resurrection of the Lord Himself. We too shall be more than conquerors of death and of hell through His deathless love.

This life will be attained 'by faith'. But by faith in what? for one cannot have faith *in vacuo*. In magnificent words the Apostle tells us what is implied in the faith of a Christian, 'I am not ashamed of the Gospel of Christ : for it is the power of God unto salvation to every one that believeth'.

A careful reading of the New Testament reveals that in the early days of the Church, it was profoundly believed that it was 'Christ *for* me' before it was 'Christ *in* me'. The two together constitute the basis of our redemption. Had there been no Christ *for* us in redeeming activity there would have been no Christ *in* us in sanctifying grace. But thanks to the death and the resurrection we now have the 'Gospel of Christ'.

Dr. Dorner in his book, *The History of Protestant Theology*, has a very remarkable sentence : 'more and more the husks which held in confinement the germinating knowledge of the significance of the atonement' were falling away. The germinating knowledge of the significance of the atonement is what Paul calls the knowledge of the Gospel of Christ, of which he was not ashamed.

Always when men grasp the significance of the fact of the atonement, although intellectually they may be at fault, it has a germinating effect upon men and churches. Is it not true to say that when the emphasis is upon 'Christ *in* us' the church does not prosper as fast as when the emphasis is upon 'Christ *for* us that He may enter *into* us'? The Methodist war-cry of 'spreading Scriptural holiness through the land', is based upon what Christ has done for us primarily, then secondarily upon what Christ can do in us.   If the writings of Paul are anything to judge by, it was a profound faith in the doctrine of 'Christ *for* me in atonement' which led to exploits in service and sanctification.

There are four very practical things about this faith which the Apostle mentions in the context, things which are worth deep consideration as a test of the fitness of our faith.

Verse 8.   The faith of the Roman Christians was a faith people knew about.   It was not a secret faith between Christ and themselves.   One of the snares of the Devil is that our faith is so personal that no one should know anything about it but ourselves.   Whosoever believeth . . . and confesseth . . . shall be saved, *c.f.* v. 12.   Faith is enriched by fellowship with other Christians.   This is one of the strongest reasons why we should support the worship and fellowship of the Church.   A child who is never allowed to play with other children often turns out to be a namby-pamby, fit for nothing; so does the discipleship of so-called believers who refuse to share fellowship with other believers.   v. 14.   If we have faith we shall become debtors (in our own hearts), and shall determine to pay off the debt by personal service for God and for man.   v. 15.   Finally, if we are ashamed of the Gospel of Christ something must be wrong with the faith we profess to have in Christ.

Let us seriously face up to that fourfold challenge, and so test our allegiance to this gigantic text: 'the just shall live by faith'.

THREE

'THERE IS NO RESPECT OF PERSONS WITH GOD'—ROM. 2^{11}

ONE of the hardest lessons which the early Church had to learn was the one enshrined in this verse, and those who refused to learn the lesson became some of the violent enemies of the Church.

The battle in the Church was practically won after Peter had been specially commissioned by the Lord to go to the house of Cornelius, and after the demonstration of the Spirit to baptise him as a member of the Church of Christ. Step by step afterwards the doors were opened to all believers, of all nationalities, and of all bloods.

The greatest *coup* of those who refused to learn this lesson of the impartiality and lack of favouritism by God, was the imprisonment of the Apostle Paul. But even in jail the spirit of Paul conquered the bigots.

The wide scope of this impartiality of the Lord is well described by the Apostle in the chapter from which our verse is taken. He first of all asserts that everybody, Jew as well as Gentile, are sinners; sinners to such an extent that all of us have placed ourselves in the place of condemnation. All sorts of means are taken nowadays to hide the reality of sin, the most widespread and insinuous being 'What wrong have I ever done to anybody?' The scriptural definition of sin, in effect, is to put our desires before the will of God. For example, I ask myself the question, 'Should I attend a prayer-meeting?' The answer may be, 'I had rather spend the time at some sport,

2

or in some pleasure, or in the garden, therefore the prayer-meeting can safely be neglected'. The word of God makes it plain that a Church apart from vital prayer will not be able to conquer evil, nor to extend the Kingdom of God. God's desire is that the Kingdom shall flourish, my desire is to engage in some sport; if the decision is self before God, the result is sin. Such a spirit is equally as wrong as that which makes a man into a confirmed drunkard. The will of God is priority number one, and anything less than that is sin.

The Apostle next tells us of the further step the Church had to take. I repeat that they were Jews, and as such were of the opinion that all the world would be condemned by the judgement of the Lord, but that the 'elect', that is, themselves, would be fully vindicated at the throne of God. 'All the world will be condemned apart from my clique and me.' It is amazing, yet true, to realize that that attitude is one of the things we have inherited from the Jewish Church. In effect, 'Myself, my family, my church, my denomination, are almost, if not quite, above reproach; but as for the rest . . . they are not worth mentioning for they are bound to go under'.

'Not so,' says the Apostle, 'the judgement of the Lord is universal.' No one can escape the fact of the judgement, for even in this matter the Lord is utterly impartial.

Jesus told us that the impartiality of the Lord is revealed inasmuch as 'He maketh His sun to rise on the evil and on the good, and sendeth rain on the just and on the unjust. For if ye love them (alone) which love ye what reward have ye?' The universal generosity of God is something to marvel at, and something to meditate upon, for it will open our mind to the immensity of the love of God as few other things can. Paul splits this lovingkindness of the Lord into three sections.

(i) 'The riches of His goodness.' These riches are well seen in the demonstration of His power in the creation and the sustaining of the universe. He spake and it was done. 'My Father worketh hitherto and I work.' Even more clearly we see them in the demonstration of His love in the life, death, and resurrection of Christ. He who went about doing good, who died to accomplish the greatest good—the reconciliation of God and man—Who lives to perpetuate His goodwill in the world, can do no other than say to the questioning disciple, 'He that hath seen Me hath seen the Father'. And in the gift of the Holy Spirit we can see the demonstration of His compassion, in the continual striving with humanity, generation after generation, for the renewal of the human race.

(ii) 'His forbearance.' The Greek word implies the delay of punishment. It is as though He hesitates to give the final blow, hoping that with a larger experience of the bitterness of sin, we may respond to His love and grace.

(iii) 'His longsuffering.' The word means the reverse of quick temper. When provoked He does not seek for swift retaliation and retribution; He waits, trusting that we shall have spit in His face for the last time.

This continual generosity, Paul continues, is designed to lead us to repentance, for the Lord knows that repentance is the parting of the ways which will determine our future destiny. The marriage of no two people would be legal if they refused to sign the matrimonial register, neither can the destiny of any man be changed from condemnation to vindication unless the pathway of repentance is trod. The whole economy of God's grace is designed with this view in mind, yet how often the riches of His goodness are despised.

Paul does not fail to bring to our notice that the same spirit of impartiality on the side of God is to be remembered by those who have repented, and are now the servants of the Lord in the work of the Kingdom. The spirit of the O.T. message, 'cursed be he that doeth the work of the Lord negligently' is immanent in the New Testament although the text itself is not quoted. We shall one day appear at the bar of Christ to answer for the way we have fulfilled our service and our ministry. What a paradox! to be justified because the riches of His goodness have led us to repentance, and to be condemned because we have failed in our loyalty to, and in our service for, Christ. Yet this aspect of His dealing with humanity cannot escape His fairness.

The secrets of men are to come to light; they are hidden in the heart, with which, and by which, we are to make a covenant with the Lord. When the heart of God was broken on the cross, the hearts of men became the determining factor in spiritual religion. The day for the outward covenant is now past. A heart-to-heart covenant with the Lord will alone bring the outward life into harmony with His will.

He is impartial in designating us all sinners, in revealing to us the fact of judgement, in the generosity of His love. He impartially demands repentance, loyalty, and a heart-to-heart covenant from us all.

Remember, God has no favourites!

FOUR

'THE REDEMPTION THAT IS IN CHRIST JESUS.'—ROM. 3^{24-26}

THIS verse takes us right into the heart of the Christian Gospel, 'being justified freely by His grace through the redemption that is in Christ Jesus'. The significance of the last two words must not be overlooked; translated into English they mean, 'the anointed Saviour', and together with the other words in the verse they take us right to the very core of the New Testament message.

The problem which the New Testament solves is as follows : man is a sinner, God is righteous, how can God forgive sinful humanity when the wages of sin is death? The answer to the problem is to be found in 'The Anointed Saviour', even Jesus Christ.

Pilate was called on to judge the Lord, and his reiterated word was, 'I find no fault in Him'. The Lord challenged His bitterest enemies in the following words, 'which of you convinceth Me of sin?'. He had done nothing worthy of death, therefore there was no personal necessity for the law of death to hold in His case. Should death have any part in His experience it could only do so on account of the loving submission of the Saviour, dying a death for some specific purpose. This is what actually happened according to the New Testament. By faith in that death so much had happened that an important and a significant explanation was demanded.

The New Testament was written by Jews, and it was inevitable that the death of Jesus was interpreted along the lines of sacrifice, for the Temple sacrifice was so important in their religion.   Different types of sacrifices had been offered for centuries, and no Jew could think of access to God without thinking along the lines of sacrifice. So it is no wonder that it was said of Christ, 'without the shedding of blood there is no remission'.   Jesus was looked upon as the Sin-offering, the One by whom propitiation had been accomplished.   '. . . Christ Jesus : whom God set forth to be a propitiation, through faith, by his blood, to shew his righteousness, because of the passing over of the sins done aforetime, in the forbearance of God; for the shewing, I say, of his righteousness at this present season : that he might himself be just, and the justifier of him that hath faith in Jesus.'

Those who trusted in the blood of the Lord soon learned that they entered into an experience which could only be described as 'reconciliation with God' : there also came into their heart a deep, divinely wrought assurance of the fact of, and the reality of, the forgiveness of sins.   Thus their experience ratified the teaching of the Lord before He ascended into heaven, and also the teaching of the Old Testament.   A threefold cord, which could not easily be broken, was in their grasp.

'He is our propitiation' they could shout, for they knew that peace and reconciliation with the God above had been secured through His death and resurrection.   He was the Mercy-seat, the place where the word of divine pardon was spoken to the penitent sinner, and where new relationships were formed.

All this came about in the individual heart by faith in His blood.   The faith of the New Testament is not what is nowadays called 'orthodox doctrine' but a repose of soul in the person of Christ; a sure calm confidence in the Son of God, as being the Anointed Saviour, and a determination to rest in His love and in His saving efficacy.

'The blood of Christ' is more than a synonym for His death. It involves the belief that the sacrificial blood of the Saviour avails for the redemption of the human soul. His life was laid down in a sacrificial death, and it was also raised up in the power of an endless life to be the fount of blessing to all who will believe.

This death, continues the Apostle, reveals the righteousness of God. It vindicates the character of God, as well as renews the character of those who will trust in its saving power. Six important things are revealed by this death :

1. It emphasises that the wages of sin, which is death, will be paid, either personally or vicariously, by every sinner in the creation. 'All have sinned', therefore, 'death is passed upon all'. And unless one personally has a sure repose of faith in Christ, and so death passes off vicariously, one must surely perish.

2. The death of such an infinite person by vicarious suffering declares to the whole world that full remission of sins can now be granted to whosoever will accept it.

3. Such a triumphant death must also involve the shattering of the power of sin, as well as of its guilt, and so looks forward to the time when sin will be vanquished from the realms of God and man.

4. The infinite sacrifice of God in Christ declares very firmly the fact that God can only deal with sinful humanity along the lines of perfect justice. 'He abideth faithful' to Himself, to His character, and to His word, even though adherence to strict justice led His Son to Calvary.

5. It also reveals the demand of the Lord for unchanging righteousness in the era of human existence.

Righteousness will determine all the dealings of God with men, and He expects righteous dealing in exchange.

6. In a word, 'His grace is revealed'—the unfailing loving regard for sinful humanity which has urged Him to go to all lengths, even to the agony of the Cross, in order to perfect His salvation for human beings. This grace triumphs over sin, death, and hell, by a generous sacrifice, inexpressible in its agony, and in its consequences.

In the year 1764, William Cowper was living in St. Albans, and entered into a period of deep conviction of sin. At length he saw his way clearly. Here are his own words : 'The happy period that was to afford me a clear opening of the free mercy of God in Christ was now arrived. I flung myself into a chair near a window, and seeing a Bible there ventured once more to apply to it for comfort and instruction. The first verse I saw was the twenty-fifth of the third of Romans. "Whom God hath set forth to be a propitiation through faith in His blood, to declare His righteousness for the remission of sins that are past through the forbearance of God." Immediately I received strength to believe it, and the full beams of the Son of Righteousness shone upon me. I saw the sufficiency of the atonement He had made, my pardon sealed in His blood, and all the fulness and completeness of His justification. Unless the Almighty arm had been under me I think I should have died with gratitude and joy. I could only look up to heaven in silent fear, overwhelmed with love and wonder.'

FIVE

ABRAHAM 'STAGGERED NOT AT THE PROMISE OF GOD
THROUGH UNBELIEF, BUT WAS STRONG IN FAITH, GIVING
GLORY TO GOD, AND BEING FULLY PERSUADED THAT WHAT
HE HAD PROMISED HE WAS ABLE ALSO TO PERFORM.'—
ROM. $4^{20\text{-}21}$

THE purpose of this chapter of the Epistle is to prove
that even the Father of the Faithful, Abraham
himself, found acceptance with the Lord, not on account
of anything he had done, but solely on account of the
faith he had in God Almighty.

We discover that the promise of God upon which
Abraham staked his faith arose out of his own need.
When he left Haran on his journey to Palestine, Abraham
was 75 years old, and although he had been married for
many years he had no children. One day he had a vision
of God, during which he expressed to the Lord his hunger
of heart for a family. In reply the Lord promised to him
such a seed as would bring a blessing to the world, a
family so numberless as the sand of the seashore, or as the
stars in heaven. The Father of the Faithful accepted that
promise, and rested himself upon it, although the difficulties were very great indeed.

On account of the old age of both Abraham and Sarah
there seemed little prospect of the promise being fulfilled.
What more natural than that he should have staggered,
wavered, doubted, or hesitated to believe, as the word
implies! Yet he looked beyond these obstacles right to

the Lord Himself. 'If He is God Almighty,' his reasoning must have been, 'then He can rise superior to these difficulties. I believe that He is Almighty, therefore I will trust and not be afraid.'

There are three types of faith, all of which coalesced in the heart of Abraham. First there is the bare act of faith, the decision to believe what the Lord has spoken. That leads to the full assurance of faith, which is sometimes described as the witness of the Lord to the soul that our faith is not in vain. Thirdly we have the habit of faith, or the life of faith—a life that is based continually on the assurance that our decision to trust in the Lord is the best thing. It is the outliving of the act of faith and the full assurance of faith.

Abraham had a faith like that, which made him trustful, and fully assured that it was no vain thing to trust in the Lord.

After a wait of about twenty years, when Sarah was about ninety years old, and Abraham about one hundred years old, Isaac was born. How tremendous must have been the rejoicing and the gratitude to God in that home when it was known that the child was safely delivered.

For twenty years, with one short break, his faith had been constant. Knowing that the faith was real and true, the Lord, even at the beginning of the period, counted his faith unto him for righteousness. He found acceptance with the Lord which involved the cleansing of sin and of the guilt thereof, plus reconciliation with God . . . all by faith. The same Gospel in the time of Abraham as in the days of the Apostle Paul, and in our own day too . . . for it most certainly is the 'eternal Gospel' of the Eternal God.

'Without faith it is impossible to please God.' Our lives need to be lived habitually by faith in God. And such a faith is dependent upon the act of faith reinforced by the witness of the Holy Spirit to the soul. Our faith must be upon the true foundation of the purposes of God in Christ.

When the time came for Moses to liberate the Israelites from Egypt, faith in the nine plagues was not enough; the tenth was the crucial one. Probably the Israelites felt like fools when they marched around Jericho day after day; yet the perseverance of their faith brought the reward. Naaman objected to the idea of washing in Jordan seven times; yet it was the seventh time which brought the cleansing.

In the year 1915, a young missionary in Lisuland contracted by faith and prayer with God for 'hundreds of families for Christ'. Five barren years passed but his faith in God was steadfast, and then in a few weeks there were over two thousand converts due to his faith and labour of love. Had Frazer of Lisuland lost hope before the five years had elapsed, the converts would never have been won.

> 'Give me the faith which can remove
> And sink the mountain to a plain;
> Give me the childlike praying love
> Which longs to build Thy house again;
> Thy love, let it my heart o'erpower
> And all my simple soul devour.'

Abraham was known to succeeding generations by two names; The Friend of God, and the Father of the Faithful. As the Friend of God he knew the Lord so intimately that he could trust Him implicitly; his confidence was based upon his friendship. Maybe if we had God as our Friend, and knew Him intimately, our faith would be stronger than it is.

SIX

'WE GLORY IN TRIBULATIONS . . . BECAUSE THE LOVE OF
GOD IS SHED ABROAD IN OUR HEARTS BY THE HOLY GHOST
WHICH IS GIVEN UNTO US.'—ROM. 5³⁻⁵

A LITTLE while ago I went to visit a lady who had
been ill for some months. All around her room was
the evidence that she was doing everything imaginable to
get better, and she confessed that several doctors had been
to see her, for she was keen to get well again. During the
conversation I was somewhat astounded to hear her say
that she looked upon her trouble as her thorn in the flesh,
provided definitely by the Lord to keep her humble, and
that accordingly she gloried in her affliction so that the
power of Christ could rest upon her (see 2 Corinth. 12).
It was quite evident that her so-called testimony was mere
balderdash and insincere. If she did accept everything
from the hands of Christ in the way she asserted, why
should she need to do everything possible to be relieved of
her illness?

The Apostle gives us to understand that our reaction to
tribulation is a test of the condition of our spiritual experience. Paul never submitted himself blindly to what
we term fate—he was a remarkable fighter against
circumstances and tribulations as being the will of God
for us.

We have a real progression of thought in these verses.
As we trust in Christ Crucified we receive justification,
peace, access, joy, and the Holy Spirit. The Holy Spirit

causes us to be born again and so become children of God, for 'if any man have not the Spirit of Christ, he is none of His'. He also sheds abroad in our heart the love of God. He does more than interpret the love of God to us, He puts God's love right in the centre of the human heart.

By faith in Christ we begin to understand something of the immensity of the love of the Lord, and of its sacrificial content. We thus begin to love God ourselves in return: 'we love Him because He first loved us'. And we also begin to love with a love like His, this working in a threefold way. We get a truer estimate of ourselves and of our true value; thus we begin to love self less. We look upon sinners as our Lord looked upon them, not so much as goats to be judged, but as sheep to be saved and brought home. Also the characteristics of Jesus are revealed more and more perfectly in our personalities.

Most of us have noticed that one of the most impressive traits in the character of the Lord is the manner in which He reacts to tribulation. Life for Jesus was full of travail, but it was always travail as seen from God's standpoint, and not from man's. That is what the Apostle means here: when the love of God is shed abroad in our hearts by the Holy Spirit, we can see life, in all its complexities, from the Godward aspect, and that is such a revolutionary aspect, that we can actually glory in tribulation, knowing that it will ripen our patience, enlarge our experience, and deepen our hope that with the Lord we shall never be put to shame.

The prophet Habakkuk could contemplate famine with perfect equanimity; 'Although the fig tree shall not blossom, neither shall fruit be in the vines; the labour of the olive shall fail, and the fields shall yield no meat: the flock shall be cut off from the fold, and there shall be no herd in the stalls: yet I will rejoice in the Lord, I will joy in the God of my salvation'. Even famine has a Godward aspect: the Scriptures give us to understand that famine is sent by the Lord for a specific purpose—accordingly even in that calamity we can rest in the reality of the Providence of God.

One of the most momentous prayer meetings in the history of Christendom took place one midnight when Paul and Silas were in Philippi. They had bleeding backs, feet in the stocks, and probably hungry stomachs, yet they had learned to see persecution from the Godward side, and so they gloried in their trouble, for the love of God was burning in their hearts. A time after Paul sent a letter to his friends in Philippi, and on fourteen occasions in a very few pages he told them to have joy, and to rejoice in the Lord. The very word 'rejoice' would remind the converts of the night the Apostle spent in their city jail.

One evening I felt impelled to go and visit a gentleman who I thought was in normal health. When I arrived in the home I found him in bed, recently returned from hospital, suffering from a cancer of the lungs. The news of the disease had entered like a bomb into the home. During conversation he told me of a text of scripture the Lord had impressed upon his mind a few days before; 'now no chastening for the present seemeth to be joyous, but grievous: nevertheless afterward it yieldeth the peaceable fruit of righteousness unto them which are exercised thereby'. The stronger the grip of the disease the harder he leaned upon that word of God . . . until his bedroom became a veritable mount of transfiguration. The Lord gave him something which enabled him to glory in his tribulation.

Tribulation worketh patience. Surely it is not by coincidence that it is James the Lord's brother who wrote, 'let patience have her perfect work, that ye may be perfect and entire, wanting nothing'. The embodiment of 'perfect patience' had lived with him for more than a quarter of a century, and he had, in that time, learned what an important element of character patience is.

'Patience worketh experience' : experience is a personal knowledge of the acts of God and man. It is a very important thing : sometimes I wish I could have started my ministry with the experience gained by a Luther, or a Wesley. But that is not God's method; His method is that experience must come from human graft, tempered by tribulation and patience.

And if we receive these things with a heart that is a repository of the love of God we shall have an ever deepening hope, an ever-enriching hope, that we shall have no cause to be ashamed, because the roots of life are hidden in, and we derive sustenance from, the depths of the love of God.

SEVEN

'AS BY ONE MAN'S DISOBEDIENCE MANY WERE MADE SINNERS; SO BY THE OBEDIENCE OF ONE SHALL MANY BE MADE RIGHTEOUS.'—ROM. 5^{19}

WE have drawn for us in this chapter a contrast between the curse of Adam and the blessings of Christ. Both men are depicted for us as the heads of two types of humanity; the one offering to us, as a natural outcome of the human race, sin, death, and condemnation; and the other offering to all who will respond by faith, salvation, life, and justification.

'When we were yet without strength . . . Christ died for the ungodly.' The connection between 'without strength', and 'the ungodly', is a very close one. We are without strength because we are ungodly; our alienation from God has caused us to enter life apart from the strength of God. The words of Paul, 'I can do all things through Christ which strengtheneth me', have a negative aspect, namely, 'there is very little I can do apart from Christ'. Which means that there is very little I can do in the strength of the first Adam.

A whisky fiend was one day piloted past the public house to an open air meeting, where he stopped to hear the singing and the message. One of the speakers lovingly asked him to seek the Saviour. The man, in anger, asked why he had been troubled, for although he hated the sins which held him in thrall, he did not possess the power to turn to the Lord. A Bible was opened at these words, 'when we were yet without strength Christ died for the ungodly', and were simply explained to the man. He grasped the words, went home, pleaded the words in prayer, and discovered that by faith in Christ sin no longer had any dominion over him. The power of cancelled sin was broken.

The first Adam brought sin into the world, but 'God commendeth His love toward us, in that, while we were yet sinners, Christ died for us'. Christ put away sin by the sacrifice of Himself, but before He can put away the sin of any individual there must be co-operation between Christ and the sinner.

This willingness to be saved by Christ is not very widespread, yet it is an indispensable element in the conversion of any person. We must come to Christ if we are to be

saved.   Christ has come as near to us as He possibly can;
He came to Calvary, and His Spirit has come to our
hearts and waits to lead us to Christ.

The work of William Booth is far better known than his
conversion; yet the work, of course, could never have been
accomplished apart from the conversion.   As a boy he
had a trading transaction with some school pals.   Not
knowing that he had deceived them they presented him
with a silver pencil case in appreciation.   The Spirit of
God pressed him for conversion, and it was borne into his
mind that he could not find salvation in Christ until he
humbled himself, and made restitution by returning the
silver pencil case.   After a struggle he did so, and
immediately entered into the glorious inheritance of the
children of God.   What a tragedy had he failed to
respond to the Last Adam.

But not only does the first Adam cause us to be sinners,
and deprive us of strength, but he also infuses a spirit of
enmity towards God into our hearts.   The Lord is never
our enemy, but somehow we can contrive so often to be
His enemy.   We often misinterpret His goodness and say
it is because He does not love us when in reality the true
explanation is because we are at enmity with the Lord,
and with His purposes.   'When we were enemies, we were
reconciled to God by the death of His Son.'

By the grace of Christ the enmity departs and a true,
deep, and lasting love for God takes its place; a holy
fellowship follows, which is the most amazing and
wonderful fellowship ever known.   A German peasant,
whose enmity had been scattered and replaced by love
was about to be operated on in Bonn.   The operation was
due to cancer on the tongue, and just before he received
the anaesthetic the surgeon said, 'this is the last chance
you will ever have to speak; if you have any important

thing to say, say it now'.   The peasant realizing that the greatest blessing he had ever received was reconciliation by Christ opened his mouth for the last time to speak, and said, 'may Jesus Christ be praised to all eternity, amen'.

'For if by one man's offence death reigned . . . they which receive . . . shall reign in life by one, Jesus Christ.'   Death, a legacy of the first Adam, is conquered by the triumph of the Last Adam.   The last enemy that shall be destroyed is death, yet it most surely will be conquered by Christ.   Death, for millions, is the last enemy; because it is the burying place of hopes and fears, joys and sorrows, enemies and friends, and finally it means extinction of the personality.   But in Christ all is changed. It is the entrance into life eternal; a Christian deathbed should always be the scene of life's greatest triumph. John Selden said in a dying hour:

'I have taken much pains to know everything that was esteemed worth knowing amongst men; but with all my disquisitions and reading nothing now remains with me to comfort me at the close of life but the passage of St. Paul, "this is a faithful saying and worthy of all acceptation, that Christ Jesus came into the world to save sinners".   To this I cleave, and herein I rest.'

So Christ strengthens us, gives us our righteousness, reconciles us to God, and enables us to conquer death : He more than liquidates the curse of Adam, for where sin abounded, grace did much more abound.   The leader of our lives must either be the first Adam (with a curse), or the Last Adam (with blessings innumerable); which shall it be?

EIGHT

'SIN SHALL NOT HAVE DOMINION OVER YOU.'—ROM. 6^{14}

SIN shall not be your lord! That is part of our inheritance in Christ. We shall no longer be domi-
neered over by sin; but, by the grace of God in Christ we
shall be able to exercise lordship over sin.

A temptation, a real snare of the devil, which so many
people succumb to, is the idea that it is quite safe to trust
in Christ as Saviour, and then to continue living a life
conformed to the sinful standards of the world. 'Shall we
continue in sin that grace may abound? God forbid!'
The story of Samson should be a warning for us all. His
hair was the symbol of his consecration to Divine service.
He played with sin in the form of Delilah, who repeatedly
endeavoured to discover why he was so strong. The
third time she asked him he began to play with his
consecration, but the fourth time he went right under the
temptation. It was only when he was in prison that he
began to learn his lesson, for 'his hair began to grow
again'. But he did finish his life supremely dedicated to
God. Yet what a tragedy his life was : his disastrous
career can be summed up in one word—compromise
(Judges, 16).

Such should not be the normal career of a consecrated
soul; we are told in v. 4 that the resurrection of Christ is
the pledge of our triumph over sin. This sharing of the
resurrection life of our Lord is emphasised time and time
again in the New Testament. There is no doubt but that

it is the basis of all Christian living. The Incarnation, the Death, and the Resurrection of Christ constitute a threefold cord which can not easily be broken, offering to us complete victory over sin.

Christ died so that the dominion of sin should be destroyed. There is no other reason adequate to explain the death of the Son of God. He came into the world to save sinners, and that could only be brought about by the destruction of sin, which involved His death.

If we are to reign over sin we must personally trust in the Christ who died upon the tree. It is vain to believe that Christ died for sinners unless we also actively believe in the efficacy of His death for ourselves. When we do that Christ intervenes by enabling us to share in the power of His resurrection : He will raise us up in newness of life.

A doctor was once complaining because he personally discovered, so he said, that the whole conception of dying to sin and rising to newness of life in Christ was all a fable. The answer he received was as follows :—'If you as a doctor were called in to see a patient suffering from a serious disease you would naturally ask him to share all the symptoms and to trust fully in your advice. After a prolonged treatment, should the patient then tell you that he had failed to reveal all the symptoms, for reasons of his own, what would you say?' The reply was, 'I should tell the man that unless he had full confidence in me, and told me all the symptoms as well as he could, that I should be unable to help him adequately. Should he persist in not trusting me fully I would advise him to get another doctor.' It is to our shame that some of us fail to tell the Great Physician all about our sins, and so put ourselves outside the pale of His saving grace. 'They that trust Him wholly, find Him wholly true.'

But this important matter does not only apply to the

commencement of our Christian discipleship, it is a life-long attitude of mind which we must adopt. It is a habit of faith in Christ which we must cultivate; we must always set Christ before our eyes. Never must we forget that sin must go by the grace of Christ; that the righteousness of the Lord must be a reality in our daily career. Never to yield unto sin is a lofty ideal; always to yield to Christ is the balancing element which brings the ideal to an earthly fulfilment. To yield to Christ will bring the strength, at all times, whereby sin shall not have dominion over us. The word of the Saviour, 'I must be about my Father's business', must be actively accepted as the principle of our living.

In v. 16 of this chapter, the Apostle reveals to us very clearly that it is a matter of either Christ and righteousness or sin and Satan. It is impossible to be in both camps. Gehazi had one of the best masters in the world. Elisha was a man of God always helping others, and Gehazi seemed to be a faithful follower. Temptation came to him after a visit of Naaman to his master, and he basely deserted the standard of loyalty to his master thinking it was in his best interests to do so. After events proved that he was wrong. How bitterly he must have repented of his selfishness! (2 Kings 5). 'No man can serve two masters.' Christ or ourselves, but not both; although we shall discover later on that by yielding to Christ we have our own best interests at heart.

And so we must continue looking to Christ that we may appropriate the virtues of his death and resurrection. We remember once visiting the Royal Worcester Porcelain Works. We followed the fortunes of the clay step by step, until the clay was unrecognisable, so wonderfully by the art of the potter and of the artist had it been transformed. It was hard to believe that the pottery, in all its glory, had once been mere clay. There did not appear to be the slightest resemblance between clay and Royal Worcester Pottery. The connection lay in the work of the artist and of the potter. Similarly, Christ can so deal with us that we become unrecognisable, as we are transformed time and time again by His grace.

NINE

'O WRETCHED MAN THAT I AM! WHO SHALL DELIVER ME FROM THE BODY OF THIS DEATH? I THANK GOD THROUGH JESUS CHRIST OUR LORD.'—ROM. 7^{24,25}

FROM the exalted statement of the Apostle in Ephesians, chap. 5, that redeemed people are the Bride of Christ, down to the teaching of Ezekiel, chap. 23, we find the illustration of matrimony—sometimes lovely and at other times not quite so beautiful—used to describe the relationship of the Saviour with the sinner. The metaphor is eternal in its significance, and remains a perpetual challenge to Christians to remain faithful to Christ in all circumstances. The story of Hosea and his wife is a type of the love of God for us; whilst the Evangelical Prophet can cry, 'thy Maker is thine husband'.

The Apostle opens the chapter by describing the relationship between a man and his wife. The law of God forbids that they should ever be unfaithful to each other; death alone can justifiably make room for a third person; until that time the obligation of faithfulness must not be broken.

Paul, as a Jew, was born under the Old Testament Law,

and as such he was wedded to it—to its commandments and to its promises. As he grew up, he realised more and more how utterly unable he was to fulfil its demands, and accordingly the more he compared his standard of living with the standards of the law the greater the sinner he realised he was. He stood self condemned.

There was no escape; even if he had renounced Jewry he could not have escaped the Law for he was wedded to it. He could not escape the consequences of rejecting the highest by accepting a lower standard of life, for it had become a matter of conscience.

Business men said the same thing during the war, and during the critical days which followed : 'there are so many rules and laws nowadays that we find it impossible to fulfil them all.' A man who spoke like that stood self-condemned; yet what could he do?

No matter how self-condemned he (Paul) was, no matter how wretched he became, he had to press on—and one day he saw what he believed was a more excellent way, even the way of Christ.

But what did he discover as a Christian? A conflict comparable with the old one, yet lifted on to a higher plane of living. Christ had a far higher standard than that of the old Jewish law, and accordingly He demanded more from his disciples. Could the Apostle live up to the standard of Christ? No! by himself he could not do so. But, 'in Christ' he found a new hope altogether, for the Saviour had a very positive contribution to make to life.

1. He discovered that Christ offered to him a full and a complete forgiveness for all offences against the laws of God and man. A good Jew, so called, and a bad Jew, so called, had one thing in common; they were alike sinners.

Whether we are Jews or Gentiles, no matter whether we are wedded to the law of the Old Testament, or to the laws of nature, or the law of any civilisation, we are all sinners alike. Self condemned or not we all fall into the same category—and Christ offers to us all a full, a free, and a perfect forgiveness. The wretchedness of guilt can be transformed into the joys of penitence by a look of faith towards Christ.

2. He next discovered that 'in Christ' was to be found a far loftier standard of morals than had ever been promulgated by any state, Jewish or pagan. The demands of the Lord were perfect love for God and for man, issuing in a life of Christlikeness. The mark of the Christian was that of love—the imitation of Christ.

But surely that only made matters worse! Not so, for

3. He discovered 'in Christ' the power of God offered to man to enable him to live up to the standard set for him by Christ. He realised that the power of God in Christ is adequate to enable anyone to live a life of perfect love.

The wretched man, the man who is made wretched by the burden of sin, of guilt, of hell, of shame, can be delivered, set free from all that makes one wretched, and from the wretchedness itself, by the grace of God in Christ. That is the glorious gospel; the fulness of the blessing of the gospel which we preach. It is another way of saying 'sin shall not have dominion over you: for ye are not under the law, but under grace'.

It is pre-eminently a message for the Church, and for the individuals who compose it. If we, as followers of the

Lamb of God, who are called to be the Bride of Christ, commit spiritual adultery, it is because, either unconsciously or deliberately, we do not draw upon the resources of God in Christ. Our Lord taught us that the adulterer must not be condemned, but should be pointed again and again to the source of true love, and to the fountain opened for sin and uncleanness.

Christian experience is many-sided and our temptations are often insidious; but let us always remember that God expects us to be as faithful to Christ as a man should be to his wife, or a wife to her husband. Yet, should we fall into sin, our Husband, who is our Maker, our Redeemer, our Saviour, our Strength, and our Guide, will say to us, 'how can I give thee up?'; 'return to the Lord . . . He will abundantly pardon', He will 'renew our strength', for God 'abideth faithful'.

TEN

'WE ARE SAVED BY HOPE . . . WE ARE MORE THAN CONQUERORS THROUGH HIM THAT LOVED US.'—ROM. $8^{24,37}$

THE whole of this chapter revolves around the two words, hope and love. The verses follow one another throbbing with a glad expectation, a sure confidence that all is bound to be well, because of the utter supremacy of the love of God. Paul brings aspect after aspect of the Christian life before his readers, assuring them that on account of the love of God their hope can abound.

We are saved by the hope that to all who are in Christ there can be no condemnation, for Christ died to deal with the sin question. Condemnation comes both externally and internally to the soul: but we are assured that when we shall stand before the judgement throne no condemnation will be passed upon us on account of the sacrifice of Christ: we are likewise assured that the inward condemnation of a sinful heart can be removed in its entirety by the grace of Christ. As darkness gives place to light, so sin is eliminated from the soul by the incoming of the fullness of the grace of the Saviour.

We are saved by the hope that Christ will make us spiritually minded. Various aspects of this spiritual life are brought prominently before us: v. 5, the Holy Spirit will eliminate sin from the soul; v. 9, the Holy Spirit will confer upon us the rights, privileges, and responsibilities of the sons of God; v. 14, we are assured that Divine guidance will not be withheld from the trusting soul; v. 15, the full assurance of faith and the witness of the Spirit will usher us into the glorious liberty of the sons of God. These viewpoints of the spiritual life are those necessary to be understood, in some degree, so that we can develop the spiritual side of our nature. We receive so much from the Holy Spirit so that we can be inspired with the hope that one day we shall be like Christ.

We are saved by the hope that Christ will grant strength for the daily task. That seems to be the meaning of v. 11, for we are in the midst of a passage which is eminently practical for this world. V. 11 is, as it were, a commentary on the passage of ancient writ, 'as thy days so shall thy strength be', also linking on to the other declaration of Paul, 'I can do all things through Christ which strengtheneth me'. The common English of this principle is expressed in the words that God not only fits the burden to the back, but that he also fits the back to the burden. We are saved day by day by the hope that

God will give strength to fulfil the purposes of His providence.

Nature presents many problems for us, and sometimes we fail to grasp the why and the wherefore, but Paul was saved by the hope that Christ will cause all nature, inanimate, animate, and human, to fulfil the purposes of God. The viewpoint of the Bible is that this world was created by God for a specific purpose, and that the introduction of sin into the human arena meant a dislocation in the working out of the purpose. It is worth while to link together, Gen. 3., Isaiah 11, Rom. 8, and Revelation 21. The argument depicted in these chapters was summed up by the Apostle in the words 'we are saved by hope'. The realm of nature, even as the heart of man, must finally be in subjection to the Lord of Glory.

We are saved by hope that Christ will answer prayer which is inspired by the Holy Spirit. The implication is, of course, that so many of our prayers are unanswered because they are not inspired by the Holy Spirit. The Spirit can pray perfectly because He knows the will of God; accordingly prayers to be answered need to be inspired by the Holy Spirit. This teaching is a Pauline paraphrase of the words of our Lord, 'If ye abide in Me, and My words abide in you, ye shall ask what ye will, and it shall be done unto you'. To abide in Christ means to live a Spirit ruled life; we shall then have the mind of Christ, which will enable us to pray in harmony with the purposes of God the Father. If we ask for what the Father delights to give then He will lovingly grant our request.

Next, we are saved by the hope that Christ is the pledge of Providence. A fourfold view of Providence is provided for us in these verses : v. 28, 'all things work together for good to them . . . who are called according to His purpose (all things work together for good to those who are in harmony with the Father of us all); v. 29, happiness is not the ideal of God for his children in this world, it is holiness, and those who supplant holiness by happiness will never be able to understand the dealings of God; v. 32, Calvary is the measure of His generosity in all things—not a petti-fogging human generosity—the purposes of God are revealed pre-eminently in the sacrifice of His Son; v. 34, the prayers of the ascended Christ for us, are a part of His providence. What a picture we have here of His providence and what a wealth of material to think about! We shall never be able to understand God's dealings with us unless we remember that His purposes must come first, holiness is necessary, Calvary is the extent of His love, and Christ is praying for us.

Lastly we are saved by the hope that Christ will enable us to secure absolute triumph over every foe on account of His love. 'We are more than conquerors'—a word imported only once into the Bible; it comes from the battlefield to describe an overwhelming triumph in war. 'He was persuaded that nothing could separate from the love of God in Christ.   He searches heaven, earth, and hell, to find something that will defeat Christ, but finds nothing —and we triumph in and with Christ.

'Now abideth faith, hope, love.'   Our hope by which we are saved is based upon the love of God in Christ; may it reinforce our faith, and determine our love, leading us to a life of utter love for Christ and for man!

ELEVEN

'I COULD WISH THAT MYSELF WERE ACCURSED FROM CHRIST FOR MY BRETHREN, MY KINSMEN ACCORDING TO THE FLESH.'
—ROM. 9^3

ST. PAUL was often denounced and was sorely troubled on account of his patriotism; although looked upon as a traitor by his fellow Jews he regarded himself as being a patriot of the highest order. What is it that makes a man into a patriot? Is it not a love for a country, often coupled with the desire that the best interests of the nation be realised? From that standpoint the Apostle surely was a patriot of the highest ideals. His enemies declared that he was a traitor because he would not allow his ideal to be debased to the level of their own patriotism.

His nation had an amazing history and tradition, which are summarised for us in vv. 4-5 of this chapter : these privileges had been unique. As a nation they had been chosen by God to fulfil a specific purpose in the world; the presence of God had been with them throughout the centuries, symbolised by the Cloud which dwelt in the Tabernacle and in the Temple; they had received the covenants of promise, the love of God had been coupled with the response of man to that love, bringing a new fellowship into being; the secrets of true spiritual worship had been revealed to them by the mouth of the prophets, priests, and kings; whilst towering above, and crowning all the other privileges was the fact that the nation had been the human source of the Messiah.

It was this last point which caused the disruption between Paul and his fellow-nationalists. They rejected the idea that Jesus of Nazareth was the Messiah; Paul was utterly convinced that Jesus was the Messiah; and, believing as he did, it was only natural for him to live as though the best interests of the nation centred around Jesus.

In vv. 6-9 he asserts that the true Israelites were those who had lived spiritual lives, living according to the covenants of promise. To be a child of Abraham was not enough, one needed to be even more than a son of Isaac; one needed to live by the promises of God. It is not enough to be born into a spiritual civilisation, one needs to appropriate the basic promises and foundation for oneself.

Such a God-infused civilisation demanded, of course, that special men should be chosen for peculiar situations. Jacob, for instance, had been chosen from amongst the sons of Isaac for the ultimate perfecting of the work of God. Whilst also, for the continuance of this work, even a man like Pharaoh needed to be raised up and utilised for the fulfilment of the purposes of God. The words, 'God hardened the heart of Pharaoh' have often been an offence. If you were to put a pile of butter into the sunshine, and also a pile of mud, both piles would react to the heat in different ways. The mud would harden, the butter would melt. So, men of diverse characters react differently to the workings of Divine Grace and providence; some hearts are melted, and some are hardened. The picture of the first Good Friday is illustrative of this.

In v. 15 the same principle is applied to the activity of the grace of God. I can think of scores of pairs of brothers who had the same parents, opportunities, circumstances, and training in spiritual worship, yet they are now as diverse in spirit and activity as it is possible to be. Why has one brother accepted the grace of God, and why has the other rejected it? The subjective reaction to those parents, opportunities, circumstances, and training, was the deciding factor. The immanence of God made one man one way, and another man another way—and each responded according to his ability. In spite of all that is said against predestination by Grace, it is a truth from which no man can escape.

In v. 21 the subject is approached from the standpoint of service for God. Why does God give one man ten talents, five to another, and only one to a third? Why does He not give everybody an equal chance? No one can say; such things are hidden in His providence.

But Paul insists throughout this chapter that all his fellow-countrymen should have endeavoured to discover just how each one should love and serve God. They had failed there. Instead of living by an active faith in God, going on step by step, from faith to faith, they had become moribund. The Lord had realised that it would happen, so, for the accomplishing of His purposes He had opened wide the doors of grace, so that the Gentiles entering in could share His blessing and His service, and work together for the perfecting of His purposes.

And true faith in God will be the determining factor as to whether any country or nation can continue to be used on a large scale for the fulfilment of the purposes of God. Jewry failed the Lord, so the centre of gravity was changed to North Africa and Asia Minor. From thence it passed to Italy; then at the time of the Reformation it passed to north west Europe (including Britain). It would now seem that the centre of activity in Christian leadership

and endeavour may soon pass from Britain and Europe
altogether—unless we Europeans respond to the grace of
God in a way other nations have failed to do in past
centuries.

Christ is the keystone. The nations which have failed
Christ spiritually, have been cast aside by Christ politic-
ally. In the last paragraph I mentioned Palestine,
North Africa, Greece, Asia Minor, Italy—all have ceased
to be numbered amongst the great powers; will a like fate
attend North West Europe and Britain? Everything will
depend upon what we intend to do with Christ.

TWELVE

'FOR WHOSOEVER SHALL CALL UPON THE NAME OF THE LORD
SHALL BE SAVED.'—ROM. 10^{13}

A STORY that was told by Paget Wilkes unfolds for
us the truth of this chapter in a very clear manner.

A clever Japanese engineer, who had a poor idea of
Christianity, but whose wife was a praying Christian, felt
the sense of conviction of sin, and decided to find relief in
meditation, for he was a confirmed Buddhist. 'Whilst
seeking to make his mind a blank he heard a voice saying,
"Believe, believe, believe." Startled, he cried out "What
shall I believe?" The voice replied, "Believe on the Lord
Jesus Christ." Deeply moved, he said, "I do believe . . .
I will believe." He told no one of his resolve until one day
a nephew, somewhat of a profligate, came in to seek his
counsel as to the reformation of his ways. He begged him
to believe on the Lord Jesus Christ. "Why," cried his

nephew, "whoever heard of such a thing? You do not believe yourself and yet you urge me to become a Christian." To this he at once replied, "But I do believe." The nephew was, however, firmly unconvinced and said, "Well, you have never made any profession of Christ, and I do not believe a man can be a real Christian unless he confesses Him openly." This appeared reasonable and Mr. T. proposed that they should go at once to a prayer meeting then being conducted at a neighbouring church, and standing up publicly confess the Saviour. His nephew demurred, but Mr. T. would take no refusal, and together they went to the meeting.

'Though unknown to the company, in the interval between the petitions he arose, and without any explanation or apology said that he wished to confess publicly that he believed in the Lord Jesus Christ as his Saviour. In the twinkling of an eye his soul was filled with joy, unspeakable and full of glory. The Holy Ghost witnessed with his spirit that he was a child of God. Almost beside himself with happiness, he testified everywhere of his Saviour.'

How could salvation and righteousness be found? That was the problem of Mr. T. Many answers are given by man to that query, but all are useless. The Jew said, fulfil the law ; the Buddhist said, by meditation; the Mohammedan said, by a blind adhesion to the Prophet; the Britisher often says, by doing no one any harm; but the Bible says, that in Christ alone can salvation and righteousness be found. 'Christ is . . . righteousness to every one that believeth.'

The need of a Saviour is worldwide, all of the remedies proposed are futile with one exception, and that one is Christ. There are even substitutes offered which are barely distinguishable from the real thing, such as the

Church, or the Bible, yet nothing but Christ is adequate. The idea that orthodoxy, either old-fashioned or up-to-date, can save, is repudiated by the Apostle in this Chapter. Christ, and nothing but Christ, is our one hope of salvation and of righteousness.

The words spoken to Mr. T. were, 'believe on the Lord Jesus Christ', and those words reveal to us the way whereby the salvation of the Lord can become effectual. 'Believe in thine heart that God hath raised Him from the dead'—believe on the fact of the Living Christ. Christ and Him crucified are never separated in the mind of Paul. The two are connected in this verse; for to believe in the resurrection of the Lord presupposes the fact of Calvary, indeed it leads on to the conception that Calvary has been consummated in triumph.

Then where is this faith to be found? Shall we need to search the heaven, the earth, or the sea? Can a man by searching find out the Almighty? There is no need to search : all one needs to do is to look into the heart of God and of man. Christ says, 'my son, give me thy heart' : man says, 'I rest in Thy heart of love'. For what is faith but the cohesion of the heart of man to that of God? the unity of two hearts which brings the fulness of the one into the emptiness of the other.

One cannot call upon Christ, v. 14, without faith; there can be no faith where there has been no word; and there can be no word of God unless it is either spoken or written, and so brought home to the individual soul. Therefore faith is the soul of man reposing upon the word of God, which will lead to spiritual intercourse.

The nephew said to Mr. T., 'I do not believe a man can be a real Christian unless he confesses Him openly'. Such a public confession is the natural result of a faith which is the union of two hearts, it is the natural outgrowth of our faith. It is universally true that a sinner must confess Christ or forsake him. You can no more be married to Christ without having witnesses to the fact, than a man and a woman can be married in the eyes of the law apart from two witnesses. To believe the contrary is nothing but a snare of the Devil. 'He that is ashamed of me, of him will I be ashamed in the presence of my Father.' Cf. Lk. 9²⁶. A public confession made in a gathering of people is not always necessary, but true faith in Christ must bring a public confession of allegiance to the Saviour sooner or later.

And the logical consequence of that confession will be Christian service. It can be said by some people of every true disciple, 'how beautiful are the feet of them that preach the gospel of peace, that bring glad tidings of good things'. Christ will be exalted by His disciples as the Fount of every blessing. The reception this message will receive will be mixed; some will accept the message, v. 20, as an unexpected blessing to be received with an open soul; to others, v. 21, it will be an unwanted and a rejected gift. Like Mr. T. we shall try to point others to Christ, that the glory of righteousness, confession, and service, may be shared by others.

THIRTEEN

'FOR OF HIM, AND THROUGH HIM, AND TO HIM, ARE ALL THINGS: TO WHOM BE GLORY FOR EVER. AMEN.'—ROM. 11³⁶

THE Apostle Paul believed that Christ is the key of all Jewish and Gentile history; even those who reject Christ are to be measured by Christ. Our Lord is the Source of all things, the Means of all things, and the Object of all things. The complex argument of Paul in this and the preceding chapters revolves around the purpose of God in Christ.

Probably an illustration or two before we deal with the argument of the Apostle will throw light upon his words. Why was it necessary for God to cause the Reformation to take place in the sixteenth century? Surely it was necessary because the best interests of the Gospel demanded that it should take place. The Roman Catholic Church had allowed the simplicity and the royalty of the Gospel of the grace of God to be lost amid the numerous accretions of the centuries. If the purposes of God were to be accomplished through the church something drastic was necessary and the Lord accordingly acted drastically.

The same argument holds good when we consider the need for the Evangelical Revival of the eighteenth century. Wesley was raised up to lead the church to a revival of early Christian experience of the grace of God. Wesley changed the face of Christendom in a manner comparable to Luther; and both were raised up so that the purposes of God in Christ could be carried a stage farther.

But it was the faithlessness of preceding generations of Christian disciples which created the need for a new departure in service for the Lord. And that leads us straight into the midst of the Apostle's argument.

The Jews were chosen by God to establish the kingdom of God through Christ. There are three aspects of this task which need to be noted. (i) The Jews were to be the recipients of the revelation of the love and of the purposes of God in order to provide the doctrinal background necessary for the understanding of the message of our Lord. Apart from a knowledge of the message of the Old Testament Jesus can neither be understood nor interpreted.

(ii) They were chosen to provide the circumstances most propitious for the birth of the Son of God. Jesus seems to fit into the circumstances provided by the Hebrew nation in a way we cannot imagine had He been born anywhere else. For instance, our Lord would have been a totally different character from what He was had He been born in either China or Britain, at the period of time in which He was actually born in Palestine.

(iii) Then, too, the message of God in Christ was of such a nature, that it needed to be universalised, and who could have done the job better than the people trained by God the Father for two thousand years? Yet they refused to accept this aspect of their service, and expressed their rebellion by rejecting the Son of God altogether.

What then was God to do? for it is against His nature to coerce workers, He always demands willing service. Did He cast off His chosen people? No! He raised up a 'New Israel' to carry on His purposes in Christ, even the gentile converts—and by so doing He by-passed the unwilling Jews. He created a new departure in the history of the Kingdom of God, even as He did at the time of the Reformation and the Evangelical Revival.

To express this enlargement of the service of God the Apostle uses the parable of the olive tree, which is a simple adaptation of the parable of the vine in St. John's Gospel, chapter 15. Our Lord describes Himself as being the true vine, and His disciples as the branches, some of whom will be cast into the fire to be burnt, and others pruned to bring forth more fruit: Paul looks upon the Church of the Old Testament as being the stem of the olive tree, and believers since Christ as being the branches; the faith of a Jewish believer *retains* him as a branch, the faith of the Gentile believer *grafts* him in as a branch; the Jew who rejects Christ is *cut off*, but if and when he repents he is *grafted in again*. Also, the Apostle adds, it is more natural to graft in again one who had been broken off, than to graft in an alien branch.

In v. 26, the Apostle confidently looks into the future to the time when Israel shall have repented, and be grafted in again to the good olive tree. They will eventually be brought in having become willing to fulfil the aspect of their calling against which they are at present rebelling.

Has God cast off His people? No! He has merely bypassed them until such a time as they will be willing to do His will. Accordingly he brings in the doxology, inspired by the remembrance of the mercy of God: 'O the depth of the riches both of the wisdom and knowledge of God! how unsearchable are His judgments, and His ways past finding out!'

Christ is the key of history; the key of Christ is the mercy of God; the key of the mercy of God is the desire of God that now in all humility men should serve Him; and Jew and Gentile alike are called to be co-heirs of the grace of God in Christ. Christ created all, controls all, and will reign supreme over all . . . to Him be glory, Amen.

FOURTEEN

'THEREFORE . . . BE NOT CONFORMED . . . BE TRANS-
FORMED . . .'—ROM. 12²

IN the light of all that Paul has said about the grace of
God in chapter after chapter of this epistle comes the
call to real personal action. 'The mercies of God' should
not make us careless and indifferent to the love of God,
but should act as spurs, urging us on to more devoted
Christian living.

The means of our transformation is by the renewing of
our mind, which follows on the surrender of our bodies
to the Lord. Actually, unless we surrender both mind
and body to the Lord, we surrender neither; for the two
are too closely bound together to be separated.

The surrender of the personality will be the means
whereby the Lord will be able to transform our lives;
which transformation is a test of the reality of our discipleship. Arising out of the surrender the Apostle reveals
how our lives are transformed in relation to ourselves, in
relation to our friends, and in relation to our enemies.

1. In relation to ourselves.

We often see an advertisement nowadays which says,
'not too much, not too little, but just right'. Those words
are a fair paraphrase of v. 3. We shall begin to get a fair
estimate of ourselves. When we have a too high opinion
of ourselves we are obnoxious; when we have too low a
view of ourselves we tend to bury our talents; it is when

we see ourselves with a transformed mind that we realize what we really are, sinners, indebted to the Lord whom we ought to serve with all our being. We shall then find our rightful place in the Church of Christ—for the New Testament always assumes that we shall be linked on to the Church if Christ has transformed us. Whether minister or layman, preacher or teacher, or a server at tables, we shall find our rightful place and serve together like one large body, every separate part working in harmony with the rest.

Also we shall find various works of mercy to attend to; works that will thrust their tentacles out beyond the scope of what is nominally called 'the Church'; and which will be a perpetuation of the Incarnation. Like our Lord we shall go about doing good.

It is not so important to see ourselves as others see us, as it is to see ourselves from the standpoint of the 'perfect will of God'. Such a viewpoint will give us the greater shaking.

2. Our relationship to our friends.

'Let love be without hypocrisy.' Pure love must always have, as a large element in it, consideration for the one loved. The deeper the love the deeper the consideration for the beloved; the shallower the consideration the less real is the love.

The love of a transformed person needs to be affectionately moulded for all on the pattern of the love in a Christian home. It will need to be respectful and mingled with humility, it will make us to be not slothful in business, fervent in spirit, and enable us to serve the Lord in all things large and small. It will reinforce our joyful hope, make us patient in tribulation, and enable us to persevere in prayer.

We shall thus become liberal in supplying the needs of others, and we shall open our homes to entertain strangers as well as friends. Sympathy will play no small part in our life, and we shall, like Christ, rejoice at Cana and weep at Bethany. Love will equalise the differences between the saints and will bind the hearts of all in the faith together.

3. Our relationship with our enemies.

We shall lose all desire for recompence; 'an eye for an eye' will lose its appeal. Honesty before all will become natural, for we shall have nothing to hide. And if we have the peace of God in our soul we shall desire to live at peace with all men. 'Vengeance is mine; I will repay, saith the Lord.' Our task is to overcome evil with good, v. 21.

David Livingstone visited the Bakaa tribe, a tribe who had a very bad name. A few years before they had killed by poison a white trader and two of his men, and had strangled a third. Livingstone was the first European who had visited them since the horrible deed, and he wanted to preach Christ to them. They were afraid of him, and many ran away. How could he win their confidence? 'Nothing I could do in the way of appearing perfectly at ease, and squatting down beside them, could remove the almost ludicrous expression of fear; until they got a dish of porridge cooked and when they saw me partake of this without distrust, the act seemed to excite their confidence, but lying down to sleep, in consequence of the fatigue of the long walk, seemed to have the full effect I desired, and they soon came round in considerable numbers.' Instead of expressing the spirit of enmity towards those who had the spirit of hatred and fear, he revealed the spirit of the love of Christ, and thereby was able to win their confidence and their friendship, which enabled him to preach the Gospel of the grace of God.

In the providence of God we do reap whatsoever we sow, but the task of the Christian with the transformed mind is to melt our enemies with kindness, and so endeavour to overcome evil with good. We may suffer if we allow Christ to transform our personalities, but we shall suffer far, far more if we refuse to allow Him to have His way.

FIFTEEN

'PUT YE ON THE LORD JESUS CHRIST.'—ROM. 13[14]

THESE words are famous, for they were the words whereby the great Augustine found rest in Christ after a long search, during which he was accompanied by the prayers of a godly mother. 'I heard from a neighbouring house a voice, as of a boy or girl, I knew not, chanting, and oft repeating, "take up and read, take up and read" . . . Checking the torment of my tears I arose, interpreting it to be no other than a command from God to open the book and read the first chapter I should find . . . I seized, opened, and in silence read that section on which my eye first fell; "not in rioting and drunkenness, not in chambering and wantonness, not in strife and envying, but put ye on the Lord Jesus Christ, and make not provision for the flesh in concupiscence". No further would I read, nor needed I, for instantly at the end of this sentence, by a light as it were of serenity infused into my heart, all the darkness of doubt vanished away.'

As with Augustine, so with others, to put on the Lord Jesus Christ involves a change in our manner of living. The Apostle here reveals how the change will make us different as a citizen, as a neighbour, and in our own personal life. No part of life is left untransformed when Christ is truly put on; the robe of salvation will affect all our being.

Our relationship to the state can best be illustrated by a reference to Christ confronting Pilate. Undoubtedly, Pilate misused the authority (which Christ declared had been given to him by God) of the state. He deliberately allowed a man, repeatedly declared to be innocent of all fault, to be executed, merely because the Governor was a timeserver and a man pleaser. Yet, the decision of Pilate, in the economy of God, was incorporated into the purposes of God in Christ. If Christ was to die as our Saviour He had to die somehow, and the Lord of glory made the wrath and the sin of man to serve and to praise Him.

That is what happened throughout history, said the Apostle. The alternative to a state governed by rulers is anarchy, which is bound to be worse for humanity than the generality of states. Accordingly the Christian who is linked on to the purposes of God in a sinful world is bound to be subject to the state. It is never right for the Christian to be a bloody revolutionary. If changes are necessary, as they must be in a sinful society, lawful means must be used to make the state into a more perfect instrument in the Divine economy. The Christian is to use peaceful methods to effect the necessary improvements.

Paul, and Jesus, tell us that we are to support the state financially. When it was announced a few years ago that Local Authorities were to be given power to raise a 6d. rate to provide theatres, etc., some Christians objected to the principle, and decided not to pay. But can we conscientiously refuse to pay the rate, because we happen to believe that there is too much pleasure in the world, while we share the blessings which the State provides with the revenues from the drink trade—which is a far worse evil than the theatre?

Our contact with the state is a relationship with a community, and next the Apostle tells us that we have a duty to individuals who compose the states of the world. That relationship is summed up in the one word 'love'. We must love our neighbours as ourselves, and by so doing fulfil the law of God. It is important to notice that we are not told to *love* the *state*, we are only told to love the *individuals* who *compose* the state.

I would like to suggest that the distinction reveals to us the occasion when it is lawful to refuse to obey the state. There are times when the Christian must say, 'we must obey God rather than man', and when we ought to go to jail rather than to submit. Cf. Acts 5. 'Love worketh no ill to his neighbour.' Every time the state commands us to work ill to another person we must refuse. Vv. 8-10 show the application of this law. No Christian, even when he is supported by the state, should ever do anything that will injure another man. Christ went about doing good, and when we have put on Christ, we of necessity must do the same.

Too, we have a duty to oneself. This is a threefold duty according to Paul.

'Let us put on the armour of light'; we automatically become a soldier of Christ when we put on Christ; and so we have the duties, responsibilities, and the privileges of a soldier, to maintain, to bear, and to enjoy. It is a warfare which demands constant vigilance if we hope to say, 'I have fought a good fight'.

'Let us walk honestly' before God and man. There must be no hypocrisy and no compromise. There is no such thing as an honest hypocrite, and a man of compromise cannot be depended upon always to put the interests of the Kingdom of God first, as we are called upon to do.

Finally we are told to do nothing to encourage sin, 'make not provision for the flesh'. The demand here is that we do not lead others into temptation, and that we ourselves do not walk into temptation and sin.

The interests of the state are the interests of God the Father, the working out of His purposes : the interests of our neighbour are the interests of Christ, the sphere of loving activity : the interests of the individual are those of the Holy Spirit, to make us and to keep us free from sin. To put on the Lord Jesus Christ is to link ourselves with the triune purposes of God Almighty.

SIXTEEN

'HAPPY IS HE THAT CONDEMNETH NOT HIMSELF.'—ROM. 14[22]

MANY people nowadays do not regard the Apostle Paul as a true guide in spiritual matters; somehow the loss of the faith in the infallibility of the Bible has brought the Apostle crashing down to the ground. 'Christ alone is our guide' is the up-to-date warcry (and quite right too). But it is not equally recognised—yet just as truly—that the teaching of Paul is a natural outgrowth of the teaching and the ministry of the Lord. In almost every way the two, Christ and Paul, stand or fall together.

In this chapter Paul is dealing with disputed questions of Christian conduct; and he solves the questions by a continual reference back to Jesus Christ. 'My sheep hear my voice, and . . . follow Me', the Lord said, and the Apostle fully accepts the principle.

In v. 4 he emphasises that all Christians are responsible only to the Master; all disputed questions as to what we ought to eat or drink, at what to play, or where to go, must be answered by a reference to this standpoint. He assures us that we must be fully persuaded in our own mind what our Lord would have us to do.

He goes on in v. 9 to tell us that we shall ultimately be judged from that standpoint. Have we or have we not lived according to the mind of Christ? Have we or have we not been rebellious against the guidance of the Spirit of Christ? Then from v. 13 onwards he tries to reveal to us just how we can apply the standpoint of Christ to disputable problems.

If you love God and your neighbour, which is the essence of the teaching of Christ, you will not deliberately do anything which will cause another person to stumble or to be hurt. Christ was very emphatic in this matter; He tells us that we should be better off were we dead rather than that we should cause a child to stumble. 'Woe to that man by whom the offence cometh.'

A little while ago I was in a home when a knock came to the door. My hostess went to the door and found a woman begging clothes for her six children. My hostess returned and told me the following : 'That woman receives 25s. each week from the government for family allow-ances; she makes it her boast that she spends the whole of the money on cigarettes—then she has the sauce to come here cadging clothes for the children.' That mother was definitely contravening the law of Christ; had the money been spent on beer, gambling, tobacco, entertainment—or any other private thing—she, by causing the children to suffer, was transgressing a law of Christ. 'It is good neither to eat flesh, nor to drink wine, nor anything whereby thy brother stumbleth, or is offended, or is made weak.'

In v. 15 he points us to the death of Christ as the crux of the matter: 'Destroy not him with thy meat for whom Christ died'. Nicodemus was unable to understand the teaching of Christ until he actually saw the Lord up on the tree; but when that happened he soon began to associate himself with the most extremely enthusiastic of the disciples. The vision of Christ Crucified revealed to him the heart of God, and he soon knew where his duty lay. May I suggest the following challenge for those who are not sure what is the Christian attitude towards disputed questions of Christian ethics? Sit in a comfortable chair and read through twice, from different Gospels, the story of the Crucifixion, and then read the second chapter of the epistle to the Philippians: and ask yourself the question, 'Why did Christ humiliate Himself and die?' Then propound the question, 'to what extent am I following His example?'

If any man can deliberately associate himself with anything that tends towards the downfall of humanity after gazing upon Christ Crucified, then he can not be a true Christian at all.

A college girl in a home for unwed mothers said the following: 'I'm not a saint, but I'm not a harlot either. I used to laugh at people who had been drinking—but not any more. In my case the tragedy it left is another human being who will never know his parents. His father will never know he is this child's father, and I have already signed him away. *It's an awful price for him to pay for my drinking.*'

Sacrifice and self control must be guiding principles in the lives of Christians.

'The Kingdom of God is not meat and drink; but righteousness, and peace, and joy in the Holy Spirit.' In other words temporal things must have a secondary place, and pre-eminence must always be given to eternal things. Our concern for righteousness, peace, and joy, ought to far outweigh our desires for material and temporal things. 'Seek ye first the Kingdom of God, and His righteousness.'

In the last analysis it all comes down to our faith in God, as revealed to us in Christ Jesus. The issue is not, 'my faith in God allows me to do so and so', but, 'I do so and so, or I refrain from doing so and so on account of my faith in God'. 'My sheep hear My voice . . . and they follow Me.'

That is faith—hearing the voice of Christ and then following Him whithersoever He leads us. Anything less than that is sin.

SEVENTEEN

'THE FULNESS OF THE BLESSING OF THE GOSPEL OF CHRIST.'
—ROM. 15^{29}

ANOTHER way of saying these words is, 'for to me to live is Christ'. When our Lord so fills and overflows the human heart that nothing alien to Christ can abide, then truly a person has the fulness of the blessing.

Maybe the best way to expound these words of the text is to work from the end to the beginning, at the same time illustrating the matter by expounding the chapter from the beginning towards the end.

Christ is the One who 'pleased not himself', yet considering who He was, the Only Begotten Son of the Father, He is the One whom we should have expected to please Himself: but from another standpoint, because He was whom He was, He was unable to please Himself. Four sentences from the Bible, spoken by, or referring to the Lord show plainly why He did not please Himself. 'I delight to do thy will, O my God.' 'Wist ye not that I must be about my Father's business?' 'The word which ye hear is not mine, but the Father's which sent Me.' Also the words spoken by the Centurion to Jesus, 'I also am a man set under authority' reveal the influence which Christ exerted, namely, He revealed that He did not live to please Himself. Pre-eminently He was a Man of God, and the chief characteristic of a man of God is that he is completely subservient to God.

Indeed He is the One who bears the brunt of our rebellion, 'The reproaches of them that reproach Thee fell on Me'. He is the One who bore our sins in His own body up to the tree.

Which leads us to the 'Gospel' of Christ—the good news of Christ. What is it? In this chapter Paul gives us a twofold view of the good news.

He came 'for the truth of God'. Most probably he means that Christ came as a Jew in order to complete the revelation of the Father which had been partially given in the history of the Lord's people, and recorded for us in the pages of the Old Testament. If any man in this world desires to know the truth of God He must turn to Jesus Christ, for 'he that hath seen me hath seen the

Father'.   It is termed 'good news' because the cry of the
human heart in all generations has been 'where might
I find Him?'; and now we can say in response, 'look to
Jesus Christ and behold Him'.

The other view of the Gospel given to us in this chapter
is that Christ came to confirm the promises of God.   'All
the promises of God in him are yea, and in him amen.'   A
few of the promises of God are quoted in vv. 9-12 : those
selected reveal to us that the grace, the lovingkindness of
God, is for all men, Jew and Gentile alike.   Whosoever
will may come and share in the tenderness of God, and
rejoice as they trust in Him.   Christ brings a revelation of
God which is universal in its scope of application and
appeal.

What may be the 'blessing' of the Gospel of Christ?
The blessings are unspeakable like the pre-eminent gift
of God Himself, but a few can be enumerated, even though
they cannot be explained in any detail.

In v. 13 we are told that joy, peace, and hope, come to
us mediated by the Holy Spirit.   In personal experience
the Holy Spirit is that element of the Godhead which
applies to human beings the blessings of the Gospel.   Joy
unspeakable, peace beyond understanding, and abound-
ing hope, are fervently desired by all, and they all come
to us from a common Source—a Source despised and
rejected by millions.

The blessing will make us patient and sympathetic
towards others, even as the Son of God is to us.   His
patience and His sympathy are unfailing, and those
virtues will only be unfailing in us, as they are received
from the Crucified.

We shall be urged to a life of sacrificial Christian
service.   Only those who have lived such a life of service
can understand what a blessing it can be.   To the out-

sider such service is foolish and futile, but to the initiated we know that it is maybe the cause of the most splendid blessing for heart and soul.

Verse 26 reminds us too that to use our money for Christ will be a pleasing experience, and again only those who give prove the reality of the words of the Lord, 'give, and it shall be given unto you; good measure, pressed down, and shaken together, and running over, shall men give into your bosom. For with the same measure that ye mete withal it shall be measured to you again'.

The apostle in v. 30 beseeches the Romans not to lose a tremendous blessing by failing to pray for the work of God being accomplished by others. Self-centred prayers are often unable to command the blessing, but prayer, real striving in prayer, will bring blessing to the one who prays as well as to the one prayed for.

It is an imposing list of blessings, and one is reminded of the hymn of Charles Wesley:

> My heart is full of Christ and longs
>   Its glorious matter to declare!
> Of Him I make my loftier songs,
>   I cannot from His praise forbear;
> My ready tongue makes haste to sing
> The glories of my heavenly King.

We cannot have Christ apart from His blessings, therefore inasmuch as we have not the fulness of the blessings we have not the fulness of Christ, and inasmuch as we have not the fulness of Christ we cannot have the fulness of the blessing of the Gospel of Christ.

Paul was full, and hoped he would remain full; some of us are empty and are content to remain empty! How appalling to remain in a state like that when we too can be full.

'Once I remember being on a glorious summer evening in a lovely garden, full of a splendour of flowers, and the young greeneries of early July, with a man born blind. And my whole heart ran out in sympathy to him, sitting there in the dark, with all that beauty around him, really there, so very near, yet for him, non-existent. And with that, perhaps reading my thoughts, he spoke of how full and good a thing life is, adding with a laugh that seeing-people always amused him with their unbelievable talk about their precious little faculty of which they make so much; but which, said he, we blind folk do not credit can really add much to the interest of things . . . And he believed that that was all that life could be.' ('*From the Edge of the Crowd*', p. 261 A. J. Gossip.) To live without the fulness of the blessing of the gospel of Christ, 'awakens that same shiver of sympathy and horror in the folk of the New Testament.'

EIGHTEEN

'I WOULD HAVE YOU WISE UNTO THAT WHICH IS GOOD, AND SIMPLE CONCERNING EVIL.'—ROM. 16[19]

WHAT would this world be like without skilfulness? It is one of the things which abides generation after generation. Whether we examine the Pyramids, a Hindu Temple, a European Cathedral, an aeroplane, or an atom bomb, skilfulness is written in large letters over all. And when Paul said that he wanted the Christians of Rome to be 'wise unto that which is good', he meant that he wanted them to be 'skilful' in Christian living, and accordingly, unsophisticated regarding the wages of sin. The history of the Church of Christ sparkles brilliantly with the life stories of those who have been skilful in the Christian life.

Three remarkable reasons are given to us in this chapter why we should endeavour to be experts in the way of the Lord. In v. 20 we are told that before long God will bruise Satan under His feet. The implication is of course that if we are colleagues of Satan then we shall share a like fate. To be crushed under the feet of God! Was it not Jesus Who said, 'The stone which the builders rejected, the same is become the head of the corner. Whosoever shall fall upon that stone shall be broken; but on whomsoever it shall fall, it will grind him to powder'? (Luke 20, vv. 17, 18).

'The grace of our Lord Jesus Christ be with you all'; that is the second reason given why we should be skilful in goodness. If the grace of Christ is with us, then we have no cause why we should not be skilled in righteousness, for the whole purpose of the grace of God is to eliminate sin from the realm of humanity.

Also, in v. 25 he tells us that our Lord is able to 'establish' the believer. This word means 'to be buttressed', to be enabled to withstand the rigours of life and circumstance. 'If God be for us, who can be against us?'

Be experts in the good!

v. 2. Stand by Phoebe, as she has stood by many others. We all know what it is to have someone to stand by us; even though at times we are compelled to say with Paul, 'no one stood with me, nevertheless the Lord stood by me and strengthened me'. Is it too much to suggest that even as the Lord had stood by Paul when he was face to face with the judge, and had strengthened him, so

Phoebe had been standing by other folk in the day of their calamity, and had been a tower of strength to them? Paul commends that spirit. Whether they did stand by Phoebe or not, we do not know; but they certainly, to their everlasting disgrace, failed to stand by Paul in the day of his trial.

v. 4. Sacrificial service has ever been regarded as a necessity in the advancement of the Kingdom, while at the same time it is often shirked by disciples. The Rich Young Ruler was desirous of obtaining the best that Jesus had to give, and so he offered himself to the Saviour. We are told that Jesus loved the young man, and asked him to make a sacrifice in order to become a disciple. The youth refused and went away grieved. He was not able to have the fulness of blessing apart from the spirit of sacrifice. The legend which identifies this Rich Young Ruler with Barnabas may be a true one—certainly Barnabas had the spirit of sacrifice which Jesus demanded, and was undoubtedly one who was an expert in discipleship. No man, unless he deny himself, can be a craftsman Christian.

v. 5. 'The church in the house'; very pregnant words! The church is where two or three are gathered together in the Name of Christ, with Christ in the midst. The level of our home life is often the level of our discipleship: the weakness of the Church is the weakness of the home. I do not believe that these words mean, exclusively, that the Apostle was sending greeting to the members of a cottage meeting (although that meaning is certainly present), but also that he was concerned about the standard of discipleship revealed in the home. If v. 5 is linked with vv. 10 and 11, this meaning becomes clearer still. Are we experts for Christ in the home, whether at worship or at our domestic affairs?

vv. 6, 9, 12. Four times we are brought face to face with the conception that to be expert in goodness, one must work hard in the Lord. Alexander Whyte used to say that prayer and hard work are the two essentials for successful Christian experience and enterprise. I fancy that he was echoing the words in this chapter. 'He that goeth forth and weepeth . . . shall doubtless come again rejoicing.'

v. 10. Apelles was a soul who was tested and found true. Skilfulness must always be tested. We do not hear very much at present of people being 'bound apprentice', but the fundamental reason why that was done, was so that no untested man could be recognised as a journeyman. The skill of a journeyman had been tested over a period of years, he had been found true, and so was able to take the status of a tradesman. The apostles had been 'bound apprentices' to the Lord; Paul had not been, and it was many years before he won his spurs. Are we apprentice Christians, journeyman Christians, or are we only unskilled men?

v. 17. Then in one word he puts the negative side of the case—avoid all dealings with those who will cause hostility in the Church, who will set stumblingblocks before fellow Christians. John puts this principle in words that are more familiar, 'love not the world, neither the things that are in the world. If any man love the world, the love of the Father is not in him'.

To make a show of Christian living and to be a colleague of Satan is hypocrisy; to receive the grace of Christ and to hold to the life of sin is not possible; to be established by Christ, and then to allow ourselves to be buttressed by unchristian folk is impossible. The challenge before us is, All for Christ and evil cast out for ever; or evil be our good and Christ cast away. There is no middle way, and so Paul makes known to the people his desire that we should be skilful in good, and ignorant of evil.

Only then shall we be able to bring the glory to God which is His due. 'Now to Him . . . to God only wise, be glory through Jesus Christ for ever. Amen.'